Free Verse Editions
Edited by Jon Thompson

SETTLERS

F. Daniel Rzicznek

Parlor Press
Anderson, South Carolina
www.parlorpress.com

Parlor Press LLC, Anderson, South Carolina, 29621

© 2019 by Parlor Press
All rights reserved.
Printed in the United States of America
S A N: 2 5 4 - 8 8 7 9

Library of Congress Cataloging-in-Publication Data on File

978-1-64317-014-5 (paperback)
978-1-64317-0215-2 (PDF)
9978-1-64317-0316-9 (ePub)

1 2 3 4 5

Cover design by Frank Cucciarre, Blink Concept & Design
Cover image: "Courtesy of the Center for Archival Collections,
  Bowling Green State University (Photograph of a field in
  Paulding County, Ohio, in the process of being cleared for
  farming. O.B. Workman Collection.)"

Parlor Press, LLC is an independent publisher of scholarly and
trade titles in print and multimedia formats. This book is available
in paperback and ebook formats from Parlor Press on the World
Wide Web at http://www.parlorpress.com or through online and
brick-and-mortar bookstores. For submission information or to
find out about Parlor Press publications, write to Parlor Press,
3015 Brackenberry Drive, Anderson, South Carolina, 29621, or
email editor@parlorpress.com.

For Amanda

Contents

Acknowledgments and Notes

These poems could not have been written without the help of many individuals and organizations. Thank you to Amanda McGuire Rzicznek, for your patience, understanding, compassion, and love. Thank you to my family—Rzicznek, Cortes, and McGuire clans—for your support and encouragement. Thank you to my extended Ohio poetry families in Kent, in Bowling Green, and points beyond. Thank you to my students and colleagues in the General Studies Writing Program and English Department at Bowling Green State University, for allowing me to make my living as a teacher of writing. Thank you to the poets who read this book in various stages of completion and offered their thoughts and reactions: Cal Freeman, Tung-Hui Hu, Gary McDowell, Amy Newman, Mary Quade, and Larissa Szporluk. Thank you to Frank Cucciarre for your expertise and willingness to collaborate (again). Thank you to the Center for Archival Studies at Jerome Library, Bowling Green State University. Thank you to Jon Thompson and David Blakesley, for your incredible support and for believing in this book. And, thank you to my enduring friends: for shelter, for victuals, and for merriment.

Thank you to the editors of the following publications in which many of these poems first appeared, sometimes in slightly different versions and/or under different titles: *Barn Owl Review, Best of the Web 2010* (Dzanc Books), *Blackbird, Brooklyn Review, Cincinnati Review, Conte, Copper Nickel, Cruel Garters, Fifth Wednesday, Forklift, Ohio, Free Verse, Ghost Town, The Great American Literary Magazine, Guernica, Isthmus, Lumina, Nashville Review, Natural Bridge, Notre Dame Review, Ocean State Review, Poecology, Profane, Talking River, Tampa Review, Transom, Tuesday: An Art Project, Waccamaw, Whiskey Island*.

Some of these poems also appeared in the chapbook *Vine River Hermitage*, published by Cooper Dillon Books. Thank you to Adam Deutsch and company for permission to include said poems here.

Thank you to the Ohio Arts Council for awarding a 2010 Individual Excellence Award to a grouping of poems from this collection.

The Devin Johnston epigraph is from *Creaturely* (Turtle Point Press, 2009).

The phrase "answer in his bill" in "Buttonwood" is borrowed from William Stafford's poem "Mr. Conscience" in *Another World Instead* (Graywolf Press, 2008).

Settlers

"Matter accrues secret history to which we are only partly privy. Our props outlast us, stubbornly persisting into new lives."

—Devin Johnston

I Dogs Without Humans

Deathless Navigator

First light, a chestnut horse
takes the shape of several swans feeding
in a field of just-cut corn.

I inhabit the woman who
watches it all through half-open blinds.

In what I think is the sky,
a self I can never know turns in her sleep.
Now the swans shrink into hackneyed dogs

but my thoughts for them are the same:
a bottoming of the senses,
a wind-weakened bridge across a merciless ditch.

The sun bruises the frost into dew.
I discover I am wholly unqualified for time—
lacking in minutes, sunsets.

Her husband enters the kitchen to slash
yesterday's box on the calendar.
A dog trots forward with down in its maw.

The sun is down—I'm surrounded by light,
enough to sweep this *me* together

and make it hold to one shape.
Centuries ago I wrote for months in this room.
The walls bled for me.

Linchpin

knows lonesome,
knows murder:

natal skulls
in late winter mud—

linchpin knows tatters,
knows *linchpin*

and a wind that kinks
tatters into braids,

hinders each, voice-
wise by the throat—

knows quiet and trees,
knows a wind like

a braid coming
dusk by dawn undone

along a heavenly stand
of pines, along lakes

where some miners
gave up (linchpins

spinning westward)
and left some tools

and crooked ruts,
ancient in the light.

Horses

One still turning to bones along the Hudson—
one returning and returning and returning.
One dragged through Pennsylvania's blood.
One waiting out a rainstorm under a willow:
one sinking to the bottom of Lake Superior.
One traded for bourbon and gunpowder—
one gives in behind a clump of sumac.
One shot behind the ear in the Everglades.
One wounded, limping through arid mountains.
One shattered on a salt flat's dark mirror.
One pushed from a cliff into the Pacific,
one seeing the world as it might have been.
One never named—left skinned in a meadow.

Taking the Mud-Cure at Willow Point

I have a black dog riding with me.
Last night's Garnacha is a talk radio
channel turned just low enough to
ignore. Soon it will be the dog's

birthday and his years will require
thought. Before sunrise I navigate
through the flattest hills on earth
where the hoped-for strangeness

expired recently, leaving a sense
of the commonplace sinking under
the weight of common boredom—
a hankering for salt-air and elevation.

The marsh is barn-dark when I rub
a dollop of mud across my forehead,
three long smudges on each cheek.
At day's inscrutable edge, I could live

contently without seeing headlights
scrape trees and brush ever again.
It's how this land offers hysterical,
human secrets, how the dog instructs

about mindfulness with only his eyes,
how I ease back into a cape of mud
while killdeer, quiet in flight, deal
their white and brown selves like cards

facedown, into the wind. Upon alighting,
their high, hilarious shrieks begin.
The sun ascends, stokes my laughter:
the clouds look exactly like mountains.

Moose Factory

There's a pattern to
it—but not a thing
repeats: an edge-town

skirting ancient water
darkness emerges through,
leaving woods emptied.

~

Two words on a map,
kin of thousands.
Place a goose flew from

to reach a southern lake
where the sky collapsed,
billowing in reflection.

~

Even the not-knowing
of a place will haunt:
anonymous riverbeds,

moon like a trout scale,
hawks resting at midday,
hunting each morning.

Cygnet

No turning from here: mills, wheels,
the big sign of the moon hangs it all.
What once was a small river—
the road is a union with my tragic forms.
Now a strap of dust, like a tongue grasped.
Don't tell me I am dead here,
drawn tight over teeth until, unknowingly,
the river grass sparkles with dew.
The roots give way and it flops.
The parents sometimes trample their young
for a moment, before growing still.
Gray feathers, awkward onyx feet,
the whole town is a hospitalized head.
My old eyes can still distinguish color.
Praying for traffic to enter the room,
a girl of thirteen, pregnant and trembling,
sucks the green medicine down.
A miner bludgeoning his wife and sobbing.
An ancient whiskey bottle tosses light.
A young man practices Bach on a cello
where the frames of row houses fell in.

Frontiertown

Cedar Point amusement park, Sandusky, Ohio

Texts are sent and received
      about the pang of gunpowder in sun.

Geese try to escape the highway
      and fail—rotting over weeks of rain.

Every noon, someone rushes out
      to check that the cannon is lit to fire.

No one reborn here ends up poor.
      Even the dogs own their clothes.

Buttonwood

I

The fish here live in the trees.
Silent along the silent banks,
Father tries for them and so do I.
A bicycle at the bottom collects
years of line, the current
drawing our backs like bowstrings.
All labor is like this: pleasing in the end.

~

Things swing to life after a night's rain:
our sinkers graze stones, roving
and scanning, reporting landward to
our hands bracing, listening. Action
into result, *okay?* Father aches
for a miracle. All day roots burrow
like tines of green forks into meat,
into earth. Spring gathers momentum.
I make a martyr of a pine branch—
the torn scent is touched and stays.
No one is hunting me down—
no one closes in. The moon pops.

~

Large water, small water, a word meaning
brain reanimated as a sort of fog.
No sleep and then more fishing,
the river piling around our boots.
A flock of psychologists, a lone
wading preacher, *answer in his bill.*
God that was a many-boned giant,
benevolent and sturgeon-calm. Images
linger in the shrine of the closed eye.

II

Older, I tip with port in the gray dawn:
two crows watching the garden,
a highway carved into a tabletop.
Sunday dinners became freak shows:
the chicken babbling in the oven,
the guests threadbare but groomed.
The photographs a week later
come up empty—that's entirely the point.
Beside it. As near as air to rain and back.
The wind is an edge Father fights.

~

The banks grow steeper—less and less
trees to spare. A film about grasses
lights my tongue. Old tile where sand
shallows, disappointment like a jacket.
Amber star: planet among the treetops.
We grow tea-full, float over gravel.

~

Late as any hour when sleep arrives,
        a bridle appears on the step. I know
it as a signal I'll sink into like water,
boots losing the feel of the ground.
There is a hole in our foundation—
months ago I plugged it with a stone.
I take a walk around our house
every morning—a storm on a marsh,
warning aimed low and fast.
Every night I dream the stone is gone.
Every morning the stone is still there.
Mother looks up through the river.

Anima

On wet sand the tracks of deer, geese,
gulls, raccoons, all appeared alien, unreadable,
until: a single set of boots.

Who is to say the water snake was not a god?

Flies adored the heads of stones half-submerged.

In the flying shadow of a dove, the catfish flexed
her whiskers, turned in her silty pool.

There were too many birds overhead to count.

Sun pressed down, a great skin over the whole river.

The smallmouth bass were voracious,
sending enormous ripples through flat shallows.

Gulls congregated on the shoals, shrieking and singing.

Something blue in the sand: lid from a jar of olives.

Something black in the air: first and last crow of evening.

There came a moment when the traffic
could not be heard, the houses could not be seen,
and I had to grasp, for awhile, at what I was.

The trees and the light crashing of their leaves—
outdone by the current's ceaseless song.

Mosquito Lake

The whole of it is old—
  black and white ducks in waves,

boards buried in the woods,
  a stranger's name stenciled.

Old rope floats around below,
  above fish in a cemetery.

The corpses progress tenderly,
  their stones young so long ago.

Potterstown

Full plot of sweet clover.
Outside the farmer's range, lost to all
on the outskirt, past the welcome sign,
back where the coyotes claim dens,
the father's tongue is a fine dust.
Population: ghosts, hawks, field mice.
The old woman will never be finished.
Anyone who loved this place has left.
Her father's haunting is eternal:
a thousand starry clasps, one by one,
more stories every morning.
Again and again the dusk snapping
and her neighbors grow to chuckling
and rolling it like a log into a river.
Every direction is a road out
taking the story of the naming,
the forsaken town hall itself a heart.
Father and child on a porch swing.
At the cold center of the compass
a word on every set of lips.
A long way to bringing him there,
down that road where the light is.

Buttermilk

You teach the morning about the body,
the body about the morning.

Thinking of buttermilk, I watch you fall asleep.

Everything we want arrives on wheels:
grass, earth where it doesn't belong, how we live,

the circumference of the circuit
crowed and squirreled by the heat,

the constant, high-crossing day, slow

as moonlight draped through our elm,
branches boiling with wasps out back.

I talk night into itself and back out.

This big elm, here well before us,
roots thicker than human legs and arms,

is dying. Neighbors stop us to comment.

We teach them candle-flicker, page by page.

We relearn the opaque surface of things.

1890

What comes to settle here stays:
thoughts about thoughts dying,

grainy moon that sweeps west,
wind drawing thin, canine strings

sideways across the creek's chaos.
I once wrote something about

the lifespans of orphaned foxes,
a charred clearing, archway of oaks

leavening distance, quick as fate.
I turn a honed thought outward

and fog sinks in, then goes—
do you know where? *It is here.*

A doe spoke from blank brush
where I had watched her go by.

I ask you again for the world.
Bring me to it again I ask you.

November Arcana

Today is the dog's birthday.
We wish him soft-focused landscapes

through living glass. Hired by
our aging landlady, they arrive

to take out two sick pines
and part of the elm.

Beauty does things by force
and all day I am away.

We agree the yard is safer this way
and go on with our aging.

All day it was the dog's birthday.
He didn't seem to give a damn.

West

Arrows comet over the hill into
a house of cards.

~

Axe stuck in a pine, left for the handle to rot; land rolling on for no
reason, for decades; no elixir half-frozen in a wormy cupboard; no
end to the grassy horizon; peeked and saw the horses growing slow; a
mosaic of gravel along some river's distended spine; woke to a thick,
human smoke; a dozen faces in the unclassified weeds.

~

The glowing hand, palm
facing you, blinks

then
stays.

Pickerel Creek

I

When the marsh surrounds it,
when the hawks come around
to it, it's nothing: five boards and a lid

balanced on a mound of reeds and
snow, eventual corpse as ballast,
brain mute as a cliff's face,

some decay kept out, some sealed in.
Swallows veer in the yellowing sky—
what is anything to anything?

Ice will melt, give. Spring will claim it.
A hundred years, a thousand years—
a face shining if the world is there.

II

Herons coming and going over islands.
What is has been slowly gathering,
lunging through tracks we've just made
in our miles and miles of nerves.
The deep snow that forces us back—
today you've been fighting it.
There's an indifference within it all
and, when walking, I see a merlin
bullet toward our street, I go cold.
Nothing has moved this way in a week,
but the whole time, we feel watched.
The untouched snow tells us to relax,
there must be a cure, a price.
What can be said? The merlin scares,
wind has kept the trappers home.
The bay is a slate of solid ice.
When I make the corner toward you
we flush a pair of geese at the far end.
The odds instruct me you'll recover
(shanties clustered off the harbor)
but there will be a day we don't. Still,
I find your complexion renewed—
the deep central ditch unfrozen, open.

III

Hawks in the snow in the marsh
along the road where nothing can end.

I only perceive them as a voice in the snow
I cannot hear, their million angles

an insistent weight. After day is drained,

plowed under, I find a steadiness
and I don't let go: a darker sliver

of belief now visible but nothing

can be seen from the center.
See now the trouble here—look again.

Here I can never inhabit one place

at one time as no singularities remain.
Snow descending for a sixth hour

and the flashing hawks still not sated.

II Untitled [for the dead]

Sweat and Steam

Thinking in the black room: clouds in treetops.

A woman I know talks me into drowning my dog.
I press his head into a bucket
and together we bury him in a suitcase.

Snow, a week, the first fly of the season.
Awake beneath thunder,
above duck and pheasant carcasses
beneath our feet. A soul.

Water hitting the basin, curtaining upward.

Hollering, cracked open with a rock,
the body spilling out onto gray sand, just
the size of a month-old pup now.
A fragmentation even of the fragments.
No reaction in the muted sea-light of things.

What now, without homecoming, without aftermath?

It all trailed me, every meal I sat down to.
A lonely holiday, wind hacking at the rooftop.
The season will not calm for two humans, a hound.

I take the earth into me, drown it
yet I remain on the earth as part.

The country wakes in the middle of early evening.
The news has been unrelenting, halting.
Places where the dead have gone, fast paths
into new names, endless skies,
negative light, no one agrees what exactly.

It can be terrifying at first, the lure
speeding back to you, making remarks

about a boulder here, a hole there
until it digs sideways into swamped timber.

The fuses blow all at once
or the meat goes bad and we eat anyway.

A bad thought down into the face of the water.
Keats is dead, did not die peacefully.

Madness outside this stillness.

The first spider of the season for three years
running has been a fat, bison-brown wolf,
its death beneath a sole a ritual.

A monastery window among rain-beaten tiles.
This is the dream I am waiting to have.
A silent place to sleep, write, read, eat, drink.
Rain on the other side of the wall,
hail pelting the glass after a long, humid day.

The season makes us unwell for weeks.

Fog mingling with wood smoke in the hills,
a constant tugging at the frayed end of logic.

Page between my hands blank as an unclaimed grave.

Unbelievable upswell of birdcall every morning.
They are the couriers of questions, asking
who will be returning and who has been lost.

I would go back, start further upriver.
Too deep to cross, crowd of anglers not so thick.
I would go so far back as to pause
at the first lamp shining before daybreak
if it would make a difference. It wouldn't.

Of Earth

Building a fire yesterday it
occurred to me to be more careful

with my hands: balance the new log
just so and new flames teethe.

~

The sun hovers downward—unsteady.
A young man steps from behind a curtain—
just starts firing. Asleep

inside sleep, I find myself wishing.
A warming day of rain pushing snow

into runoff greening the grasses,
pooling to send clear sky back
at itself—birds hitting moths at dusk.

~

Every forest began as a fire.

Of Hindrance

No faces yet for the dead—
no names, places, or certainties.

The little dog in the soul sits
cocking his head at the newscasters.

No faces yet for the wounded.
Little dog goes mad, howling now

for the million languages to answer:
which has a word for snow-

on-pines-and-the-wind-
banging-like-a-dull-axe-chopping?

An overwhelming majority of
headwounds. Glass bowl

of naval oranges—wrecked trees
outside the hospital windows.

~

There is a narrow stretch where
the current slows over gravel and shale.

It is a popular place to cross.

Of Travel

A public storm coming together
in a brain under fluorescent lights:

a wind primed to lift you
by the ankles and into the drink,

the rain fat and calm, steady.
It makes a monster of the river

and once I got so sick in the boat
I had to sleep on the shore,

woke staring at the red Roman numeral
one where the dog's eyetooth

caught my left hand—

is the door into sunrise so small?

Of Hardship

I cannot explain the vision I had
this morning beside a fatherly oak—

(onlookers rushing in every direction—
smoke below the lecture hall's

pocked ceiling (how it feels—or,
how I imagine it?) and the quick,

caustic tang—burnt powder
rich as speech, but no understanding

onward through blood-dark
stitchings of brush, rain, and reed

resisting. Tiny lanterns of pain.
To make the burden bearable

I speak or even sing into the gloom
as I walk, my shoulders burning

sweetly apart, smoke in the air).
Nothing I couldn't understand in it.

Of Current

Every *where* is a ceaseless center—
the black S.W.A.T. uniforms

(a series of centers colliding)
hustling like magnets through spring snow,

into perpetuity. Behind each ripple,
blood driving in circles—behind

the blood, loud drums: cars
pounding by on an overpass

with me waist-deep underneath.

(No walleyes to show for the morning—
cold as it is, the turbid river, its pulse.)

A high bridge in higher wind:
all of meaning up there going by.

The Body Sat Waiting for an Afternoon

It was late in the age, in light snowfall,
when the ear of the desert inverted silence
and a dog's inherited memory of fire
poured like the north wind through my ears.

I feel no need to question it. Hence: trust.

At dusk the sands cool, distant yips
echo around the hotel room: empty cans, cigarettes,
rough comet trolling across being's wake,
the small sounds dogs make in the night.

I need coherence but I need to reject it.

Four hours to the border for a closer look:
dogs find the body intended for raptors
halfway between island-tomb and oasis,
ice thawing, reduced to bruised grass underneath.

I . . . must I start with I? Things are nervous.

White hands of the sea—deep underbody
in the unending musty sprawl of the tombs.
Bodies ran wordless at spirits crossing forward—
the vultures and eagles profiting regardless.

I take it all back—forward then reversed,

the body waiting for huge, gangly shadows,
tense souls making footsteps far beneath it.
Dogs trot north into half-naked lowlands.
After scenting blood, they are difficult to dissuade.

Of Religion

Each being: an instrument of His?
The herons chase minnows at

His behest? The dog fights
his new harness (one strap

behind the ears, loop around nose)
to teach us some new tricks

regarding anger and patience?
Consider this our world's center:

roiling, balled-up mass of
tentacle upon tentacle, a sideways

globe-sized eye—

~

The second before the gunman
makes his intentions believable:

there—that face—no happiness.
Understanding is nothing more

than the brain at the middle of it
all, peacefully asleep.

~

Are we, then, the dream?

Of Season

Wayfarer. What I call the bug

that dogs my students—weak fever,
smudge on the throat's rosy altar.

We are a drawn bow and we are
the arrow and the target too.

I admit all the misery in this place
won't be turned by it. *Wanderer.*

⁓

The floor trembles. Or, the earth?

Through matted, dew-fed grass—
painstakingly, sweet and stinging—

flowers press furled heads, their
roots drawing strength from a corpse.

A rough-legged hawk wheels south-
east. A fathom above her, pintails

speed north, thinking as a flock.

⁓

Most of us get better but some, never.

Of Opposites

We call the dog a pig, but
in the most affectionate manner—

it's the grunts he grunts
when lifted one place to another

or tempted with a bite of kibble,
little red drum thumping

in his ribcage's fluttering dancehall.
On one side of this, the blood-tempo beating,

on the other: dark overspray of matter
as the gunman turns the barrel on himself.

(Stand up, frightened boy-ghost,
test the balance of your alien boat.)

Is he drifting, rowing, a bit of both?
A door inside a door inside a room:

sand-fine ice hurries into banks, drifts—
early March, of course. The bottom-dregs.

Of History

The news has drifted far:
numbers, dates, photographs.

In the stillness, a violence
of feathered brigades unmooring

against the roseate mercury
of sunrise. *It's ugly.* Beneath, silence

braces as the birds load
song after song into the morning—

so like peering down a walk
overtaken by low, wooly fog

(a mob of unlucky silhouettes,
little else) that the river takes me

right down: downright, drives one knee
into shale, leaves a hand

groping after a split-second sense
of balance on the bottom.

~

When has water ever missed an entrance?

Of Burial

This is me, trying to understand:
spatter in all directions.

But in two weeks the news
relents, lurches sideways into what

will be forgotten within the month.
Scavengers hoist torn shadows

away over hilltops. Beneath
those hills, imagine a crawl,

a torch gnawing the walls:
bones of men, frames of eagles—

the remains intermingled.
All this time the weeping continues

as snow renegotiates the tension
yoking blossom to blaze,

gracing oaken gullies,
shaking the new myth by the throat.

Houses, Drifting

In this house
we are offered cannons, armor, reprieve
against sundown
sweeping the battlefield

clean. A blue-black heron (lord
of birds) swoops close,
rending the air in the ears of unanxious corpses
    around which

the details of spring have emerged:

off-white moths among white dogwood petals.

        ~

      In this house we
are robed in pond-weeds—
the soles of the feet scrubbed,
eyes stitched shut with corn silk.

From the wall a voice skewers our pasts
an act at a time.
The struggle for the door is tremendous,

the blind mob breaking one another
into jaws, legs, heads.

        ~

In this house we find the low
groves where we were born. A man wrestles

a wheelbarrow from the river's fluid din—
does not notice us

gaunt as winter, braying

for human recognition.

And in this next house we float about
in Victorian nightclothes,

scowls of portraits visible, dimly,
through incandescent torsos.

The kerosene lamps
saunter by now and then,
pinning the ghosts back with laughter
while rain flies in
                    through an open
                    window.

In this, in this, we find ourselves outside dignity,
taking to the contortions that first held us.

Four winds for the tossing of limbs—
blood withdrawing from pools of stain,

        the light waking back up.

In this one, here,
suddenly around us, we are offered
the still center disemboweled
        from the cyclone's gray dervish,

a view on the cruelest of absolutes: places
torn raw, lakes and rivers
        brimming with selves.

But that cannot be all.

On a thread of sun, we ascend
straight into the territory of theory.

Of Energy

Like mile on mile of pines
underwater, the dead,

shoulder to shoulder, breathe
the cold, depthless air.

Music of the present life:
yellow crash of a house party

two blocks south—I flick
a wet leaf in the rain, feel

a ghost stir in my ankle,
rushing for the heart's gate.

A pause, late at the reservoir's
crowded edge. Acid-blue sod

underfoot. Counting the months
backward, a ringing chanting

sparked in the nose and throat by
the daisies heaped into a vase: deep

headache that ravages the night's
rest. A fresh noise spins the dog

upright in our bed. *Someone is trying,*
you whisper, *the back door . . .* I'm out

like a weapon: empty lawn, patient

stars, vibrant groundswell of birds,
revelers singing in the distance.

No water for miles.

Of Progress

I look out over lawns, quaintness—
the dead still very much invisible

but it's said the Great Black Swamp
sucked horses down by the team,

turned the harshest pioneer souls
into thin idiots begging for the end.

No stasis here in the raw turning—
for a century, it has been dry.

~

Once there were only questions.
Now in that direction: free-

ways, cities, towns, abandoned
outlet malls, the right seeds

for growing desperation. *Inside him,
this murderer, no regard,*

not even for the self. Handfuls of trees
have survived. Harassed by a west

wind, their leaves take many shapes
but never those of faces grieving.

Of Memorial

So they smashed one (it had
been a cross)

thinking that one less would
change something.

*The boy's story is already a gone
thing—a spent match.*

~

Strange, ornate doorways, winters
slung low with unlit yards

& wet, slack sails, successive
gardens ringing limestone fountains—

the sun rolls back: a round door.
This spring, the fullest of moons is

yet another door, the anteroom beyond
scented with gunpowder and bowels.

(*He's that nearby—
wandering among the migraines.*)

~

The universe swallows him. Doesn't blink.

Grand Army of the Republic Highway

The final world where each face
rises from a pool of sweet mint
and rotting salmon: a death-stilling sunburst
behind what lasts an exact instant.
Mother Nature grows absent and
this trembling—
big Norwegian maple leaves along
their way in the wind kneel to it.

The shrill alarm,
soft, nearly otherworldly,
of a drake wood duck as it flushes,
grazes the peeling siding.

Not far from here, railroad tracks.

⁓

Two somersaults and goodbye
to the drake in the cold hair of trees.
Deer after deer in the ditches—

up and down Route 6 in Ohio
the snowmelt drawing back unveils

unrepeatable hieroglyphs, strange in
how the limbs all splay
in equally unnerving directions.

The sky is drained of the body's shadows
until point
of view delicately collapses, history's
mindless stewpot boiling unattended:

the forests taken down into
boarded-over shopping centers.

~

The *I* has been extinct for centuries,
its roads claiming layers of name.

The patient blacks out at exactly
daybreak, shuddering.

~

Not far from here, railroad tracks,
barely identifiable beneath brush,

wait through what has gradually leapt
up and through them: wild aisles half-
thick with surrounding woods.

A traitor, grim among the proletariat,
envisions how to end it all
while forty miles south a horse-huge
engine lugs boxcars onward.

Of the Universe

Blood and air
collude,
vessels split into galaxies of rust,

the body's economy rejects
defeat,
demons of the contemporary

demand their stubborn cycle:
terror, outrage, and mourning.

An eventual hardheartedness
dyes the skin from inside

to match the incomprehensible
where
the moment's business

is chasing the always-bad dog,
his quicksilver bliss aspiring

(wool glove in his jaws)

to give the ongoing shock pause.

(I slip—crush finger under knee
but forgive him

and for a moment
it saves me.)

III A Map of Vine River

Cul-de-Sac

The brown and white spaniel bit.
      Rob's mom said I deserved it.

Thoughts through an empty head:
      summer on a bike,

round, round, to the right—
      reeling, through the universe.

Children adore outer space—
      so much of it is left.

Little Portage

His dog makes a circle in the grass,
the gulls and killdeer
                    crying and crying.

It was me, although I couldn't have been there—
I know the place only from a map.

He sits and sees the current moving,
the light thin and tough like the sleek
light over Lake Erie.

                    Nothing can astound
him. The light goes on dividing intently,

untangling a yellow resolution from violet.
At first he thinks of it as rain, then

a fragment tuned to a larger thought,

a ghost he can see standing off by itself.

Laudanum

When it came down to it, it was sleep that woke him, and he found
it silly, the calendar beside the nightstand, its forward and forward
(never backward) of square, blank days.

~

To migrate, must I the dark
or the light?
                    Granite polished,
flowers spitting pollen. The eating,
           the sobbing.

~

                  Home funeral,
fragrant coma. *Break the ground.*

             Napkins touched to mouths.

~

To let a pipe leak long enough to cause a bulge in the stairway wall.
To come to it sitting alone in an armchair with an oil of two swans
flying a garish dusk over the mantle. To dull the pangs of a season
with an incredibly small television.

~

               Every motion to come
hangs wave-smooth among his atoms,
         against pain
             and back
to it. Being: an end to it.
          Stop aiming.

His photos and slides arranged in drawers—his cameras, stereos, reel-to-reels, microphones, electric boat motors, handmade televisions—gathered for it in a dusty bedroom.

What leaves, goes:
>> a certainty.

Stars remain.
>> From west to east
a wind rises, failsafe and terrifying. *Accept it.*

Five dumpster-loads later and the place more tomblike than before. The people at the open house shed a bit of their futures in each room as they pass through—a crowd of travelers waiting on the two o'clock ferry. A luminous crumb of *it.*

What stays is mine. Hawk-shroud,
>> souls from a quiver,
>>>> a footing
in the river's stones.
>> *Singing voices, stop. Hear me.*

There was an old bottle of it, the label barely legible, sunlight fogged by the basement windows, a printed map of the county, property lines and all, from 1952—a painting of father and son hunting rabbits through the decades of dust.

Killbuck

Farm on farm sank forward.
We grew happy without knowing
through heart-smothering fog
and suddenly, the highway.
The detour unraveled—a new
pig shed, apple barrel, spade.
One road led to an older one—
nothing but further farms,
then to gravel, then to dirt.
My father and I pressed on
to a two-lane straightening
through cattails and marsh stink,
into towns dark for the night,
the route, a flashlight snaking,
a single gas station ablaze.
Away, my brother made it:
a horse in the clouds, barely awake.
Nothing inherent here. Miles,
then the sprawling graveyard.

Ikon

Hazed-in cities of her present days,
these weak hours insist on us.
At the ends of our winters, we
all have at least one of her.

There is something more to say:
we are never here—a stillness
in the fog-lit cities of our pasts.

In the clatter of heels on damp stone,
she is always there in motion.
Now we can't stop thinking of her
and she has been ignoring us.

There is yet even more to say.
It is that these cloudy hours
at the end of the winter are her time
to pocket one of each of us.

An open sky, the empty moon,
specks of geese or crows crossing
her face as it envelops us.

Geomancy

The feathered saints of evening flit
down through the wooded hills to construe
salads of hailstones and leaf-wreckage,
the thunder having sped east-northeast
toward open water after leaving nothing
altered in the major features below.
The angle of river can always guide
a dumb soul or two to welcoming fields
where struggling plantlings yearn
for breath to sweep their leaves, enter
a rough, black portal at the thin roots.
A young crop of beans: stationary
ferry to a strange, coppery existence.
A good dog can scout this scent for miles
over mountain fog and village cookfires.
The wind is a color she can deduce
a million intimations from, unflinchingly.
The same wind comes to the saints, as if
they were abandoned boats on a wide bay
when the clouds pass and the chop slows
to a pulse, the shore a long mouth
that hasn't shifted expression in years.
All things that find a death there take
an invisible token of that freshwater pout:
a bone is dragged into pines and oaks,
an organ ends up sailing around in the rain,
the rest is dissected there on the sands.
High song in high branches—a sane
nothing that will happen until it ends.

Sidecut

An eternity of shapes crossed among trees—
at one point the face sank toward us
then froze the clearing with a damp glow.
No raptors blurred among the higher branches.
Afterward the eyes closed and the mouth closed,
pushed up into the unbroken, hard-lit woods.
The pierced palms gestured without moving,
the window-sized chunks of ice in piles, the slit
in his torso swallowing willows and wrack.
How were we to hear it in the backwater,
a syllable of fire and a syllable of thaw?
How does the stretched current reach us at all
through cardinals springing like beads of blood?

The absence of colorless light in the world
as the dog locks stares with a half-tame doe.
Once the small herd disperses we can smell
their odor still thick and feral around us—
the sting of hair and a thousand wise daybreaks.
The river under the ice keeps at its pulsing—
runners split the air with huge white breaths,
the water frantic and static, breakneck yet calm.
Each move of the wind tames like a lash.
Once more his face opens featureless eyes—
each footfall a move against the cold light,
each being a shadow swinging over snow.
The thorns tipped above us and then were still.

By His Own Hand

Between us a sense of bridges becoming trees,
a rope singing itself into a noose, stones
in the desert that have never been turned—
sometimes the terror of being satisfies,
the house fades into sequoia-huge shadows,
and night grows longer around it, no longer
around your neck, but
                              around longing itself.
In the stream's boiling, headlong mystery
some faces look like those of working animals,
some eagle-like, most barely human at all.
No telling the lengths you have taken,
can't pretend to know your deepest notes:
the yowls of a dog with its leash caught—
the chattering of china shards on metal.

In the stream's jammed-up branches and stones,
through nights of unzipping rain-white roads,
here's what I've been writing: empty windows.
More like facts than when you first saw them.

The slack-jawed moonlight.
                              Within the static,
your memories are made more distinct,
but through the fluid doorways we call day
I'm striving, distant one, to be abstract.

Kelleys Island, November

The mainland's ghost sends up an old light
as we leave for morning in the ghost's boat.
Mimicking his winter motions in darkness,

Erie rocks toward the ghost, then away.
We put on the ghost's clothes, wear his face—
our wake cuts the crossing's gray stare.

Ghosts stone-quick, swift and whistling,
ghosts with sparks in their evergreen blood:
buffleheads—goldeneyes—broadbills—

when the ghosts arrive we stand still.
The process: a ghost—the outcome: ghosts,
Pelee Island a waxen smudge in the north.

We trick the ghosts into not hearing us.
Huge underwater rocks gather tree-ghosts,
moss-smoke, and glare flame-thin below.

Deep wave-ghosts flock by the hundred—
the quickest blink among their ghost-families.
When we sleep here the voices cease.

When we coax the ghost into our trust,
a thousand ghost-limbs merge with daybreak.
We know ourselves by hunting such light.

A Map of Vine River

I

He holds the map up to the mountainside,
a thing in the sky turning to earth.
To be a map of a face without lines,
to be a turning thing in the sky.
A line on the map means hunger—
a room filled with mounted deer and birds.
What she fears is the totem of anything.

All maps lead to and from the *here*.
She preferred pines groaning in the wind—
when they move from there, long ripples.
The maps were bright, although blank.
Nothing could be said for their cheerfulness,
no center would do, no heart would match.
A named place indicates days passing by.

Late, they heard bridges dying in the cold.
Silent faces at the end of dinner.
He was not talking to her, but to himself.
Blood at the mouth's northern edge.
Their years together became something true.
A moose came knocking snow from boughs
and she stopped making words for real things.

II

Any line could be the last, the end.
Starlight will not do, moonlight will not do.
For a brief time, nothing else appears

until a hunger stalks through the birches:
an Earth in the sky seen from afar,
a mark on the legend meaning *chateau.*

Inside itself, a map has no boundaries.
The scruffy face lunging between bars,
a run of loose gravel and dirt in the woods.

He was wrapping a dead horse in maps,
mud and grit on the southernmost hoof.
The face is a map with infinite lines.

Long ripples and loud music on the lake.
Days passing by indicate destiny slowing,
remains taking on the challenge of decay.

It was sleep that made a center here.
Apart from them, surrounding them: *else*—
to be a real word among the gone things.

His yelling shocked her into believing him.
There was a moment when they came to—
she called and called to it all afternoon.

III

A mark in the legend meaning *strangeness*:
owls swoop from one line to the next,
a small key turning behind her eyes.
She let the meaning take itself for granted.
The map is a hunger for dimension,
what meaning becomes becomes meaning.
He preferred the abstract view from indoors
and within the chateau he found maps:
a goat at the local fair, giddy and loud,
three ghosts holding hands in the lane.
She knew one hillside from another in sleep
and she was part of a lake, a subtraction.
Later, in a restless sleep, they spoke of it,
seeing the illusions come and go at will.
Bobbing in the marshy end: silent faces—
each night a new voice made itself known,
the maps coming loose and flapping away.
Both of them together under cloud-light.
Bother the animals and they will lunge.
He could feel anger rushing in his legs.
What they could see of it blinded them.

Vine River Charter

This field always was bright.
       Geese, never. Only robins,

coyotes. A cupful of marsh,
       vodka-trees—heaped:

a sheet thrown off in a fit.
       The houses have backed off,

track of a walker in sand
       who took only one step.

Shivaree

In the chapel tonight a word was read—
in the white chapel on the green, a word

bounced on oak and pine as it was read
in a room in the midst of a swamp

that settlers drained dry years ago
then filled in enough to anchor a town

where a white chapel was raised and stood,
stands now with this word rising through it,

ghost-etchings of marsh oak and cattail
nodding in the sanctuary's ringing air,

the hum of humanity, the audience listening
or pretending to listen, merely present

though two went together into starlight,
the word with them, then echoing ahead.

Punderson Lake

Sunlit ghosts at the kettle-lake's bottom
    bring rain, bring shade

where I sat cross-legged in the boat,
    silence of wave after wave,

silver can of beer under my shirt.
    Shrewd trout, rainbow-scaled,

a series of clouds linked through centuries,
    arriving in our names.

We were enough to keep each other up for days,
    the land beginning as *everything*—

three years living apart until finally
    the gulls squealed something human

above the cabins and beach—the mill,
    its golden-green turning of utter meaning.

It would be a full week until we met again.
    I have written your name in the lake—

in a corridor of ripples and leaves,
    in vibrations dulled under years of stone.

Sleep eluded us, the night outrunning us.
    On the other shore—here and under:

years east of radio waves, sirens, hours before
    shapes of lean animals thinking

headlong into woods at your touch
    waking through me, your body rushing

beneath my hands, waking where ices
    crush all of existence down to pith.

Ethic

The sky begrudges
space for our roof—
night
makes room for more of itself.

~

Before dawn near the underground river; woman to her neck in silver
armor; dark coast of long hair as she bends; levels a longbow at steel-
head in current; arrows just one and rises to leave; the wind wakes me
even after my burial here; a clean passion.

~

     (It was like going neither forward
     nor backward in time—

     like
     not caring.)

Bluegrass Island

Oaks on one side of the river.
      Oaks on the other.

Wind through the brick factory,
      grass soldiering on.

Little gray dog nesting
      where a deer endured dreaming.

Even the sacred trophies sleep
      the sleep of anything.

Verge Escapement

A love changing, but without tense:
it begins with a spring dusk,
the earth they existed with,
the rawness of winter receding.
Just the thoughts they believed
giving way to deeper quiet.
No death for that room of sun.
Birds moving north, waters rising
to speak clearly about truth:
the land racing itself by months.
She is still impossible for him—
a completion always dissolving.
He comes closer to things now:
the movements never as perfect
as the *always* that became them.
Rains, gradual and green, emerge.
Parts of them, even now, haven't left
to bring gardens back around
from which neither of them turned
and the sky pink with evening—
a sea of constant, happy light
ripe for silhouettes of birds.
That afternoon sits apart—a spark,
things gradually coming awake
and nothing to do but lock and unlock.
The end: a coupling that means
the mountains draped with snow,
dog-eared pages stained with wine.
For what feels like a lifetime
he goes even further and finds
the world is always in time:
things full-grown for the winter
they crossed above during walks.
He goes back to the long, deep river,
afternoons of unlocking each other:
a movement with infinite variations

and it was straight to the bed
then a day that does not warm
until finally mountains appeared.
The rain ages and feels like snow—
hours of farms, trees, rivers
and suddenly the green is white.
A writing of letters to and fro
and brown is gray, the moon blind.
It broke her fears into threes.
But this blindness has an end
that doubled them with joy.
The loose cycle still will repeat:
the hand-in-hand strangeness
despite the moves against it.
They begin with their first months.
Things are open to amazement.

The Light at Willow Point

You-know-who
              stayed at home today.

His daily bread is lambmeal
                        and bones—
his skull the land's last meal. Like mine.

        I intended for this all
to be positive,
                a chance among the lilacs
to glimpse nature slicing forward

with a random truce,
                        its infinite limbs
extended, the air ghost-thick
                        with mongrels
time has winnowed into species.

Each breath counts:
        you-know-who slapping his tail
in sleep, miles away—

                        the heron's turning—
the clumsy stoop of a harrier into cattails.
        Take bone.
                Take eye.
                        Take heart.
This marsh polishes memory
                        like any other,
our testing of order
                        always a confirmation:
the wind rowing the wide bay

brisk with dusk.
                Be glad for it. Go home.

About the Author

F. Daniel Rzicznek's previous collections of poetry are *Divination Machine* (Free Verse Editions/Parlor Press) and *Neck of the World* (Utah State University Press), as well as four chapbooks, most recently *Live Feeds* (Epiphany Editions). He is coeditor of *The Rose Metal Press Field Guide to Prose Poetry: Contemporary Poets in Discussion and Practice* (Rose Metal Press). Rzicznek teaches writing at Bowling Green State University in Bowling Green, Ohio.

Photograph of the author by
John Jarvis Used by permission.

Free Verse Editions

Edited by Jon Thompson

Pilgrimly by Siobhán Scarry

Poems from above the Hill & Selected Work by Ashur Etwebi, translated
    by Brenda Hillman & Diallah Haidar

The Prison Poems by Miguel Hernández, translated by Michael Smith

Puppet Wardrobe by Daniel Tiffany

Quarry by Carolyn Guinzio

remanence by Boyer Rickel

Rumor by Elizabeth Robinson

Settlers by F. Daniel Rzicznek

Signs Following by Ger Killeen

Small Sillion by Joshua McKinney

Split the Crow by Sarah Sousa

Spine by Carolyn Guinzio

Spool by Matthew Cooperman

Summoned by Guillevic, translated by Monique Chefdor &
    Stella Harvey

Sunshine Wound by L. S. Klatt

System and Population by Christopher Sindt

These Beautiful Limits by Thomas Lisk

They Who Saw the Deep by Geraldine Monk

The Thinking Eye by Jennifer Atkinson

This History That Just Happened by Hannah Craig

An Unchanging Blue: Selected Poems 1962–1975 by Rolf Dieter
    Brinkmann, translated by Mark Terrill

Under the Quick by Molly Bendall

Verge by Morgan Lucas Schuldt

The Wash by Adam Clay

We'll See by Georges Godeau, translated by Kathleen McGookey

What Stillness Illuminated by Yermiyahu Ahron Taub

Winter Journey [Viaggio d'inverno] by Attilio Bertolucci, translated by
    Nicholas Benson

Wonder Rooms by Allison Funk

Lightning Source UK Ltd.
Milton Keynes UK
UKHW040800280219
338027UK00001B/65/P

9 781643 170145